Blood Lies: Race Trait(or)

poems by

Karla Brundage

Finishing Line Press
Georgetown, Kentucky

Blood Lies: Race Trait(or)

Copyright © 2024 by Karla Brundage
ISBN 979-8-88838-425-1 First Edition
All rights reserved under International and Pan-American Copyright Conventions. No part of this book may be reproduced in any manner whatsoever without written permission from the publisher, except in the case of brief quotations embodied in critical articles and reviews.

ACKNOWLEDGMENTS

The author wishes to thank the publications in which poem in this collection previously appeared.

Ishmael Reed Publishing Company: "Wanna Be White Girl." (2007).

sPARKLE & bLINK: "Alabama Dirt" (2020). Nominated for Pushcart Prize

Nervous Ghost Press: "Sister Solidarity—Suspend your Belief" "Reflections on Lady T" (2020).

A selection of these poems were published in a chapbook, *Mulatta—Not So Tragic,* Fleur du Mal Press (2021).

Wall + Response Broadside: "Ten Points" (2021).

Publisher: Leah Huete de Maines
Editor: Christen Kincaid
Cover Art: Robert Fischer
Author Photo: : "Photo TaSin Sabir" of Karla Brundage at the Morcom Rose Garden, Oakland CA. www.tasinsabir.com
Cover Design: Elizabeth Maines McCleavy

Order online: www.finishinglinepress.com
         also available on amazon.com

Author inquiries and mail orders:
Finishing Line Press
PO Box 1626
Georgetown, Kentucky 40324
USA

Contents

Context Cultural 1

Wanna be White Girl 2

The Great American Experiment Part 1967 5

Open Wound 6

Both, And 7

mule: myo͞ol/ 8

Quadroon (noun) 9

Quadroon (Active) 10

She's a Mulatto 11

Inheritance 12

Memories 13

Quadroon (Passive) 15

Octoroon (Definition in Process) 16

Alabama Dirt 17

What is Betrayal and How did it Change you? 19

Suck on ice 20

Who are you and whom do you love Black woman? 21

Forms 22

Noun and Adjective 23

Compounds 24

Not to be confused with Moor 25

Octoroon 26

Octoroon: (noun) 27

Greedy Mouth 28

Mixed 30

High Yellow Gal 31

Suspend your Belief 33

One-drop rule 35

Double D Standard	36
Mammy	37
Underneath	38
Conquered	41
April 13—NGO Speak	43
She Dreams a 10 Point Plan	44
Sub Urban Monologues	45
Internal reality of situations I find myself in—on the phone with my dad	47
Expats in Africa	48
Chatting up Black men at Lake Merritt	50
Quicksand	51
Go all the way in	52
Advice from Married Women	53
My Black Body	55
Back to the topic of the word whore	57
Behind her back	58
Not White Enough, My Brother	59
Angela	60
Why do Black People Protest?	61
Define: Wild Yellowtail Sushi	62
Race Commandments	63

The book is dedicated to the liminal state of Alabama

If any white person and any negro, or the descendant of any negro to the third generation, inclusive, though one ancestor of each generation was a white person, intermarry or live in adultery or fornication with each other, each of them must, on conviction, be imprisoned in the penitentiary or sentenced to hard labor for the county for not less than two nor more than seven years.
    Alabama anti miscegenation statute Section 4184,
    Pace v. Alabama, 106 U.S. 583 (1883)

Context Cultural

This world is full of contradictions
        internal and external.

Sometimes the external contradictions are
  complicated by internal contradictions.
Sometimes the internal are complicated
      by the external contradictions.

One job of the poet
    ████████ is to shed light
              on these contradictions.

I choose to do so though the examination of my divided
      self
           my Black body and my white body.

Sometimes I rage rage against my black body
Sometimes I pity her.
Sometimes rage rage against my white body
Sometimes I pity her.

Metaphorically it's important to make an inquiry
My Mother inhabits black body
My Father a white body

Under which label will you prefer to
submit my mental health record?

Wanna be White Girl

I was a white girl once
who dreamed of riding a Harley Davidson
and drinking vodka straight
while leaning over a pool table
tattoo on my ankle
that said property of...

I was a white girl
who had white friends
and white boyfriends
who loved me and
drank with me
locked me in closets
told racial jokes and
then apologized.

We drank gin and tonic
and roamed the streets
looking for trouble
because it never did seem to come to us.

I was white
yes
I was white
and I wore torn blue jeans and tie dye
I listened to the Rolling Stones
and Lynyrd Skynyrd
I lived the words and knew the pain they held.

When I was white I dreamed of being
Old Home Days Queen
at the county fair
where music was real
and women wore cowboy boots
I had my Stetson and my
Buck knife.

I danced the two step
and played Bingo on Saturday nights.

When I was white I loved a man
named Cincinnatus who drove a Harley
flew colors, and lived in West Virginia.
We drank every type of liquor all
mixed up into one
danced to country music
and fell out the door when it was time to go.
When we fought
it was violent
but I loved him like I have never loved.

I rode in fast cars listening to The Who
asking "WHO are you?"

But I was white
I was.
I was in on the secrets
the truths the lies,
the only problem was
that people kept mistaking me for being
Hawaiian or Chinese
Palestinian
or Black.

So I looked in the mirror and saw
my skin is brown
my hair is brown
my eyes are brown
and I wondered…
Where did god go wrong?
Because being a white girl
trapped in a Black body
is no small mistake
and the stress was beginning to take its toll.

So, I killed that white girl that I once was
I stopped her life with one clean swipe.
No more Led Zeppelin
No more white boyfriends
No more dreams of making my brown eyes blue.

But I was a white girl once,
you wouldn't know it by looking
that once dreamed of drinking vodka
straight while laying back on a pool table
tattoo on my ankle that said
property of…

The Great American Experiment Part 1967

1967 often times referred to as
The Summer of Love-ing vs Virginia
        Paisley neon hippies making love in the bushes on Telegraph Avenue
                crocheted bikinis naked chests
                      kneading love not war.

An American colloquialism
        a further melting of the pot,
                three witches cackle mixing ingredients and out pops me.

Miscegenation
        Free love
                Afros uncut hippie hair.

Acid orgy of boundary breakers
        change the system by willing subjugation of white semen
                and that stuff that women ejaculate that has no name

Age of Aquarius

End of miscegenation law: July 12, 1967

Open Wound

Scars inside the body
protect themselves. Vines of veins
        rooted in my lower belly.

Insert tiny scissors. Cut
out the overgrowth. Snip
up pieces. Return to blood
stream tiny pieces of me.

Ancient places were lovers
(now strangers) trod or trampled,
laughed, maybe kissed
weeded over.

Forests of vines
strangle the womb
of future life
extricate and remove.

Erase a footprint
leave a scar
erase the memory
admit a vast blank.

Both, And

Mulatto:
of mixed breed
young mule
a half-ass.

Of mixed race
two segregated halves of privilege and want.

Socially acceptable and degraded.

Mulatta: feminine

Kept in the Big House for breeding: Mulatress
irrevocably composite, hysterical and rigid,
so-called black and so-called white.

Old English: *Sunderboren* "born of disparate parents."

Related Entries: Mule

mule: myo͞ol/

offspring of a beast of burden and a stud

1.   a hybrid plant or animal, especially a sterile one.

"De nigger woman is de mule uh de world so fur as Ah can see."
Zora Neale Hurston

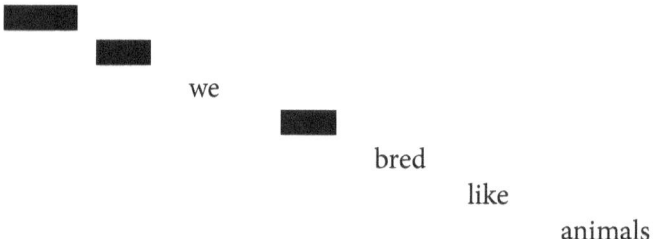

                we
                                bred
                                        like
                                                animals

Quadroon (noun)

1707, "offspring of a white and a mulatto," from
Spanish *cuarteron* (used chiefly of the offspring of a
European and a mestizo), literally "one who has a
fourth" (Negro blood), from *cuarto* "fourth," from Latin
quartus (see quart), so called because he or she has
one quarter African blood. Altered by influence of words in *quadr-*.

This can be explained as having one Negro grandparent
or two grandparents who were octoroons
but who's counting?

America is counting...
counting slaves, counting bodies
counting profit
counting drops and one drop counts
One Drop of African blood
makes you legally a Negro in 1707

Constitutes three fourths a man.

Quadroon (Active)

Fragments of bloodlines
she walks the quad before sun rises
flashes of memory
shoulders squeezed between angry thumbs.

She desired to be held
but not
down, muffled scream
a bang on the door.
Lock in.

Now she weaves her way home
hair matted in semen
cold prickles shiver her bare thighs.
Night's sequined dress
a drape.

She's a Mulatto

I am so glad they said that you did not have freckles and that your hair was not red we did not know how you would turn out your hair is so straight so good hair I am so relieved you have good hair and not hair like your mother's but we did not want you to be confused who would you identify with who would you be who would you marry I mean you would not really be black and you would not really be white we were worried you would be confused and we did not want you to have to choose one over the other you would have to be both

glad they said…we did not know…your hair is so straight…so relieved…you have good…hair not like your mother's…confused…identify…marry…not black…not white…worried…choose…both

not marry…not black not white…worried…choose

both

and

Inheritance

When I was born my daddy left me
white tiger stalking my back

his gift was to be worn like a cloak
of invisibility
rendering me power and less

I spent my library time trying
to prove him wrong but walked right into a baby with
broken water calling kettles and searching for black.

There was no way to break all the Morse code of
my identity to smash the mosaic walls mattressing my thoughts.

Coming full circle now he is right
that cloak he gave me fit
that stereotype is all I have
I keep her with me in the form of his best intentions.

When I was born my dad gave me a stereotype
told me that the Minstrel show was the truth
my existence was the only lie.

He left me to sort it out and retreated into his own
White sorrow—took his inheritance and
bought himself a punishing hermitage.

A very white thing to do
to retrieve the lost inheritance
to buy the land
to want to give it leave it to his white son.
In the end
that did not happen.

I spent my whole life trying to prove him wrong
to prove my mommy and I were not Jezabel
that Black men not all named Tom or Buck.

Memories

In 1966, my mother's first cousin Sammy Younge Jr. was shot and killed in Macon County Alabama for using a "White Only" bathroom.

Blue green shag carpet rubs damps upon my skin
cement bricks for bookshelves
planks of unvarnished wood sag under the weight of
Hair soundtrack over and over .. "ain't got no.."

My face is always near the floor
belly down.

Drugs in the house- part of our fundamental belief in freedom.

I am good at occupying myself.

Grown-ups fighting for liberation.

We don't talk about him.

Sammy- high yellow
well educated
Tuskegee boy
Middle Class Negros from Alabama
rich as some whites
more educated surely.

Before we were hippies, my family is conservative

Army and Navy
Bay of Pigs

Comes home to Alabama sweet
Whites Only

He marches
He joins SNCC
He follows the rules of revolution

But one night
he doesn't

What was he thinking
going after that old man?

Curls matted with blood
golfclub still
clenched in his hand.

II

(Boy!)

I ain't no boy

(C'ain't you read
Whites Only!)

What you gonna do shoot me?

Shots in the dark
blood oozes from open wound
in back of head

He sees Cuba
Naval whites.
He sees himself
holding his gun.

Urine releases itself
into pavement
with brain matter, blood.

A seven year old girl
named me
stares at this photographed image

captured after his
spirit floated
into the half moonlit sky.

Quadroon (Passive)

Latin _____Spanish_____Spanish_____French
Negro offspring of White and Mulatto
One quarter Negro blood:
      (still enslaved but, may
      be in the Big House)

Octoroon (Definition in Process)

Grandpa is a Black Indian.
His parents 14th Amendment certified
      full persons
Black Indians: 1/2 Native American and ½ Black
So if grandpa's parents were Powhatan and Black
      Grandma is building back the black blood
Are you mulatto?
Then you marry Black
Are your children are ¾?
but the word is now African American.
Then maybe they marry out
division causes erasure
lines in my math
grey smudge in ivory parchment
my theory no longer a proof.

Alabama Dirt

never tasted Alabama soil
phloem clay
it's the dust I'm made of

sweet tomatoes
Uncle Sam bowed
under the sun
gently handles the small fruit

so few men in my
family line
live

family secret
buried in denials

Sammy lies in a pool of my mind
golf club in hand of blood

I call my mom on the phone to ask
about vigilante justice in
the segregated south

we don't talk about that

but was there justice?
I ask

time follows no rules
and gun shots still deafen
as a child I was obsessed
with a black and white photo—I'd hide in
the corner and go over it
in my mind

lay in the bed with Sammy Younge Jr.
dreaming him to smile

what made him decide to fight his battle alone
at night
in Macon County
after participating always as part of a team

you had emotional problems
mother says,
back then
I just did not want to talk about it

all the things she does not want to
talk about
my emotional problems she calls
them

images of blood still pooling on
Black cement
imagined weapon
justification
for death

was it in his beautiful head
that they found the bullet
college educated brains shot out
for being hot headed, uppity

ripples of this one death
penetrate generations

here I am still
swallowing pills

What is betrayal and how did it change you?

It comes from that which you love most
surprise slice of a knife
razor in the tub
a slip, when chopping tomatoes.

In darkness
asleep in the warm bed of trust
dogs come for your flesh
eyes watch and wait
icicle to the heart.

A skinny girl stands naked on the stage
lights shine on her bare skin.

Suck on ice

"No suh, i mean yes suh"

This is what he says when

White hand places a dominant sneer on my shoulder
"Hey boy...whacha doing here with this pretty nigger girl?"

Fish clam fingers linger on my cheek whispering lust

"Aren't you going to share her with me
—With us?"

Cardboard body
Adrenalin, drinks forgotten

We cannot speak
Shame hangs images of
Unspoken rememories

"Why didn't you protect me?"
Words form spit on my chin, i lay my head on his chest

Trees murmur gently to one another in the
Warm summer breeze

Who are you and who do you love Black woman?

My heart is at the dog's belly. Lying in the street, blood.
No one returned to pick it up.
A man with curly brown hair dead.

A silver heel
Slamming of metal doors

I went home that night and all the
Glasses fell off the shelves.
You could see right through me to the other side.
I told you not to go there, daughter said.

Forms

15 mulatow, 15 mulliato, 16 mallatto, 16 melotto, 16 molata, 16 molato, 16 mollotto, 16 molotto, 16 mulata, 16 mulato, 16 muletto, 16 17 malatta, 16 17 mallatto (N. Amer.), 16 17 mullato (N. Amer.), 16–17 malato, 16–17 molatto, 16–17 moletto, 16–17 mullatto, 16–mulatto, 17 malotto, 17 melatto, 17 molater, 17 moletta, 17 mulleto (Sc.), 17 (N. Amer.) 18 (U.S.) malatto, 17–18 mulattoe, 19–malata (Jamaican), 19–mulatta (Caribbean), 19–mulattoo (Jamaican).

Noun and Adjective

Noun: A person having one white and one black parent;

                                                          a hybrid;

                                                                                         a green sandstone;

                                                                                                                         a chili

Adjective: Of tawny skin

Compounds

mulatto bitch, mulatto tragic, mulatto confused, mulatto hair

mulatto jack, mulatto boy, mulatto girl running wild on the rocky shore

mulatto loam, mulatto land, mulatto soil…

mulatto trees murmur gently to one another in warm summer breeze

Not to be confused with Moor

    (though I often am)

Moor 1: Open uncultivated wild
An Othello of untamed beauty
"A moor preserved for shooting"
A wasteland.

Moor 2: Mixed of Berber and Arab descent
Muslim and Moroccan
North African.

Moor 3: Scattered and then
Tied to a dock
Tethered
Sold.

More:

North Africans do not
identify as Black.
Some do not claim African.
Protected by the white sands of the Sahara
a short boat ride from Spain
them claim nation
not Continent.

Berbers are AfroAsiatic
Self Named Mazighen
Free people

Octoroon

Offspring of Quadroon and
White
One eighth Negro blood (still not free—but maybe passes sometimes)

Daughters of rape we are

Mulatto-mother + white father=

Quadroon mother + white father=

Octoroon-mother + white father=

> Don't let them all be my children please
> I want to own them
> Not love them

Octoroon: (noun)

There also was some use in 19c. of
quintroon (from Spanish *quinteron*) "one who is fifth in
descent from a Negro; one who has one-sixteenth Negro blood."

"quadroon". *Online Etymology Dictionary.* Douglas Harper, Historian. 6
Feb. 2017. <Dictionary.com http://www.dictionary.com/browse/quadroon>

Grandpa is one half Native American but embodies black
Grandma lives black but presents as white
What is my mom?
And me
I am ½ that plus
1 whole white
My two grandparents maybe add up to one full
Black grandparent
So am I a quadroon?
Great Grandma Maude is quadroon, her mom mulatto, her grandma French.

Octoroon?

Why then, do they call out Mulatto?

My daughter

Mulatto+Black =Sambo

Greedy Mouth

Cut my scalp onto this cloth.
Take my head wrap dripping blood
wrap it into your own.
Wear my skin like you own it.

Place these beads from my waist into
your ears. Excavate my eggs and eat them
on your plate as a garnish.
Palate your tongue with
sugar from my clitoris.
Garnish your wrist
with the smallest bone of
my left toe.

Wrest the air from my lungs
into the plastic bottle
between your knuckles.
Rest your fake hair on my chest.

Here you can play the doll
of your hatred housed in
lockless doors with golden
coins in a locked chest.
Sever the locks from
my scalp and wrap them in
a song you shout in the
wind. Coin your winnings

in the key-locked vault.
Wind the coinage in your sad
sad heart. I am nothing but a finger
Thumb.

You have taken my scalp and my spine
my voice and my mind.
I have emptied all for you
who have opened your greedy, greedy
mouth to swallow.

Mixed

Miscellaneous elements
Mingling soils—Melungeon
Of foreign father or two
Fraternizing
In love with an-other
Tri-racial isolate
Thrown into confusion
Bloodless
Countryless
Tragic

High Yellow Gal

I arrive in New York City
La di da di
close to the edge and
without a radio

Suitcase in perpetual hand to
create an identity from leis and cowboys hat
teddy bear, tiger tattoo
fragments of racialized body

A trunk full of India ink for my homemade tattoo
segregated clothing wrapped in wishes from
20 years ago.

Outside Grand Central Station
rush hundreds of New Yorkers dressed in black.

Born in Berkeley via New York Germanic WASP and
Alabama Jack and Jill
Ethnational cultracial pan-diasporic
Multi/bi/dual

New York is no place for standing—
a foreign food that no one can name.

II

Vassar College 1985

Ladidadi

White they are—
what does that mean to me in 1985?

He locked me in a phone booth and told me it was my fault and he
was not unlike the other who locked in his basement naked after I lost
at strip poker or the one that called me small brain and tried to make
me think I was crazy. He told me it was my fault that he just fucked

me and couldn't I see, because I was beautiful, not just beautiful but exotic
and did I know what that did to men?

Grandmaster Flash is singing—Don't touch me cuz
I'm close to the edge
I'm trying not to lose my—

III

Standing in front of the mirror
I am nearly bald
I want to be ugly, really ugly.
I tell everybody
my name is Spot.

I stop speaking.
People I have slept with
don't recognize me without.
Hair.

I learn how to hide
to walk in shadows
Black women there
see me.

I had to cut it off, I say.
Believe me sistah
I know.

Black girl hair is a burden
straight or nappy
permed or natural
it is always a statement
resistance against something.

An act of defiance is waking up and looking at myself.

Suspend your Belief

So when you look at Melania, and then Michelle,
you have to ask- where is sister solidarity?

I mean they never pretended to have it
I am talking about you and me the audience.

We watched for the past 200 years, First Ladies
who have had to undergo the double standard

(not the double D standard)

of perfection and family values.
Now we have Melania.

She is ..well
What is she? (being mixed I can ask that question)

Is she a victim of sexual trauma? Is she a sex worker?
Does she have rights? Is she a whore? Is she a gold digger?

Is she an airhead? Is she an immigrant? Is she a sellout?
Is she a survivor? Is she smart or is she dumb?

Is she leveraging her power? Does she love her son?
Is she a schemer? Is she a ghetto girl?

How did she get here? Was she just waiting for the
Old fart to die? Is she surprised? Is she happy to

be forced to wear turtlenecks every day?
Is she relieved not to have to use her tits as collateral?

I loved Michelle, don't get me wrong
Michelle stood for everything I have aspired to be…

She was the dream princess for most Black women
She was the 1%, she gave us hope that Black men

are attainable for us…

She had to work harder, be stronger, be straighter
take more shit, talk better, be more perfect than

any other First Lady ever…ever… ever was
We know her story. We get it. But, like Melania

I still use my tits for collateral. I am a victim of sex trauma
have been called a whore, and would take that old man

for all I could, if I had the balls to. Sometimes I am a ghetto
Bitch. I still live alone. I wore turtlenecks for a lot of years

to atone for my past. That's why Melania can exercise
her free speech and advertise "I don't care, Do you?"

That is why Michelle is still writing books
to inspire us to "take the high ground."

One-drop rule

Is the propensity to be raped
inherited?

Statistics say yes.
Read the bodies of the
women in my family:

Dis
Cover (naked should I explain)

Great Grandma (murdered)
Grandma (what did she witness?)
Mama (by gunpoint)
Me (it was between friends)

Where do we log the names of
those whose bodies have
been violated?

Hips pressed against a wailing wall

Double D Standard

No one has asked if she has had an abortion
How much do you want to bet the answer is yes

No one has asked for her birth certificate?
No need to, it's so obvious.

Swallowing comes easy to her, pride, insults
And bodily fluids, spit, tears, and saliva

She knows, that anyone who looks at her
Sees straight through her clothing—she is

Always naked. I know—I looked at the photos
Online and now, she is always naked to me too

Mammy

After 25 years he thanks me…

I hold the aftermath
This is a placeholder.
After my daughters father called to thank me
for being a dedicated mom
when I feel dried out
useless
sterile
so the thing is..
this Mammy poem will connect to the Mule poem

Underneath

Underneath her veil is Victoria's Secret
I see a glimpse in Dubai's great mall
where I partake in shopping
until 2 am.

Historic Ghanaian castle in Accra
known for its role in the slave trade
sold to Cedecom
a German Corporation.

China's international road building monopoly
leads to mining of silicon
and breast implants?
Oops! Wrong veil.

Low caste Indians expatriate to Dubai
performing slave-like labor
wage discrepancies reflecting lightness
of skin

Expatriates lounge in Hammam
take Zumba at the gym.

Anyone who has means hires a maid
or brings in a girl relative from the country.

Underneath the dashiki is Calvin Klein
I don't really care- I'm just sayin'
I'm probably wearing some right now.

The first man to visit me after I was born was
Eldridge Cleaver and his wife Kathleen

I remember drawing castles with Angela Davis
laying in her lap while my mom gave a speech.

Hair is bought and sold
faster than ice cream

It's supposed to be Black hair
But it is from India

Hindu women sacrifice their hair
for the upkeep to Taj Mahal.

Taj Mahal the Black blues singer
Lived in Hawaii- married white- Anna

I don't care bout that either
I'm just saying- I know of their mixed race kids
It's not so simple, you know.

Koreans cornered the market of Indian hair
sold to Ghanaians, Nigerian, Abidjanaise
Black women do the braiding

The black market sells all things i
iphone, ipad, itunes, and of course
US Dollars at ½ the price

Underneath her white robe is a role of
Benjamins

Underneath that smile is a look of
scorn

That traditional print headscarf
was made in China.
Yes, the mud cloth, too.

Leader in production of cocoa and coffee
Ivorian farmers can afford neither.
Many have never tasted chocolate.

Businessmen of every nation
sweat in full suits and ties.
Underneath is their greed.

Soldiers who carry AK47's slung casually across chests
offer to carry my groceries, open my car door
walk me to the car singing.

Underneath is a young man from the country
making money for the first time.

Underneath may be a killer.

We come to class each day
books in hand,
What is underneath?

Conquered

4 hundreds
years Christians
trekked thousand$ of miles
bearing bibles and long winded
sleeves

choking Malian warriors with
ties
strapping down Xulu breasts
un cinching waist-beads to trade
in the Americas for land
replacing them with girdles
and full length skirts

Hawaiian tongues cut out
2 pronounced hymns
with high lace collars

hair unbraided
into tangled heaps called
Nappy
un-locked and pressed, ironed
clamped
wrapped
hidden

Christians
come in long lines with hard
heeled boots
kicking in doors
shoring knee-high woolen socks

pants replace ceremony
to manhood
with submission
shorts assimilate

In more modern warfare
The Christians undress their enemy

promoting bare heads
free flowing hair
breast liberation in bikinis
tattoos and appropriate native piercings
Even waist beads re-emerge   without ritual

April 13—NGO Speak

Target population
Recruitment
Enroll enlist register
Units of service
Units served
Hours served
At Risk Population
Take a shot
Underserved
Displaced
Underrepresented
Facility use permit
Site rental
Miss our target number
Hit our target
Trigger word
Trigger warning

She Dreams a 10 Point Plan

> *"...an immediate end to police brutality and the murder of Black people."*
> (Huey Newton)

1. The brutal killing of Black people must stop. Children
2. are not meant to be hungry. Give them lunch and... Freedom
3. Schools that teach self-determination and... Community
4. Employment is a right, not jails. Close them and stop police
5. wars of aggression that support unjust laws in this land .
6. We need bread, education, justice, peace, control of new
7. Technology should make healthcare completely free too. We
8. demand prison reform and reform to so-called crimes under unjust laws
9. to carry arms to protect ourselves and power to determine
10. Our destiny is not robbery by Capitalists but Unity.

Sub Urban Monologues

The white women are gathered
around table of pink champagne like labias
wearing no shoes

Chatter tinkles from pristine facades
an outsider, I am let in
because today we all have Vaginas

There are only 3 husbands attend
a banker, the mayor, chief of police
they circulate preening feathers

Monologues on women's sexual freedom
toss terms like #metoo movement
clitoris and shame, freedom and power

metoo metoo…I want to connect, but withdraw
Instead of solidarity I hear
metoo metoo

Me too, too… me, too, I have secrets
protect those I love from exposure, too
In 1855 Carolyn Bryant Donham lied

Condemning Emmett Till
In 2015 we lose Freddie Gray
For *reckless eyeballing*

Later that day,
I attend the Black History Month
Gala and minstrel show
A room full of Black faces singing
Carry me back to Old Virginny
1880's celebration
dancing soft shoe
strumming the old banjo.

This page is intentionally left blank in honor of the dead.
It is a statement against the senseless killing of Black women
in America and women globally.

Internal reality of situations I find myself in—on the phone with my dad

my dad's caregiver
has to navigate
the wild
within him

the manifest destiny
brokeback mountain
Marlboro man of
Lehua flowers and propane
refrigeration
ice cold showers
a generator that makes noise

From a far—I navigate two landscapes
physical and emotional
Is it safe to keep my father there
his beard past his chest

Soiled diapers and rat excrement
How far does one go to grant
someone their last wish

Expats in Africa

skin alabaster shining
                        I see her walking from a distance
                                  Dust road—dirt plasters her white legs
They told us not to wear shorts
                for 6 months I have covered my shoulders
against
        to protect
blue sky
           white woman arrives uncovered, unaware,
                     shoulders beckoning solicitations giving all
                                  western women whispered label whore

little suns
dance
water down dusty path
shoulders bare
in defiance

I cannot
        allow myself the freedom to
                      dress how I want—so European/So American to
                              arrive and not respect the culture

To be in her
skin allows
freedom
to defy all tradition or
embrace it as her own

My own thoughts swirl manically in my head.
        Back in the Motherland and still I am not free.

Voices of "respect" your elders and "respect" the culture—you are not an outsider here you will finally belong.

But I don't.

Her womb carries

the white skin the
right tone to shadow
over darkness

How can she walk in this culture with bare legs? She is safe always safe.

She walks easily in danger.

Every footstep
A grave

Chatting up Black men at Lake Merritt

black tights
unable to quench
      her curiosity
she's so fresh and fit

flirts with lake merritt dreaded drummers
flashing fifties
money free flowing like her locks

imagine her in three years jogging
three tan/beige/brown children in dual seated stroller
chatting with the other baby mamas

Black women stay home
walk in groups
the way we are told
avoiding eye contact

simmering inside

the trick is old
but she never fails

Quicksand

Charbel from Lebanon said:

>Keep both hands on the wheel
>press hard on the gas
>when driving in deep sand.
>If you turn the wheel
>you get stuck.
>
>Don't avoid the sand
>Go through it.
>
>Your whole instinct says
>drive around it, but you gotta
>go through it.

Go all the way in

My father is crying on the phone
In my heart urge arises uncontrollable

Life all smashed into one tone
knots in a voice box
knife through the Adam's apple.

I will peel the skin
from the bottom of my feet
to stop your tears
the closing of your throat.

Advice from Married Women

It's hard work to be in a marriage
    Code for—I'm lying to you right now
    Code for—Even the most devoted seeming couples are unfaithful
    Code for—we are here holding hands, but at home we tear each others eyes out

Beyonce and J-Z—Infidelity is a part of life and makes great art (I mean babies)

I'm one of the hardest workers I know
    Code for—don't have time for a man
    12 hour work days
    raised my daughter alone—too strong they would say—you need to learn to compromise
    Never enough I say back—never ever enough
    3 college degrees, bought a house, all these things take work
    but nothing takes work like a man.

When I ask my friends the secret of their happy marriages
    Hard work they say
    I work hard, I work hard and it's hard
    to trust
    we wont leave

Hard work in marriage
    Lies I think—mostly lying to your friends
    Telling me to accept nothing but the best, when your partner does not match you
    Telling me to marry someone who is my equal, when you have supported your husband for 26 years
    Telling me to demand respect—when really—what does that mean?
    Demanding respect is about the only way I know to stay single your entire life

Work hard is
    Accepting infidelity
    Being able to be lose face
    Taking someone back after they did the worst possible thing you can imagine
    Paying all the bills and not asking for anything in return

Going to events alone
Sleeping in separate beds
Hating each other most of the time
This is working hard and all of it is the opposite of what people tell you to do

My Black Body

This is my body
my vessel
in it a memory

Come inside and take a look
the blood that remains
circulating in mass media
on display.

We are the gurus you look for
the incarnation of a mammy
embraced and then transformed

I claim it.
I claim the caregiver
humble servant of
children and elders

Back bent over tubs of water
washing always
cleansing

Refining and redefining
bills and bank statements
editing and co-opting terms.

This body holds scars recent and past
scars from penetration of
whips, tools and medical devices.

This is my body.

Pushing out children to
be protected and nourished.
Holding them in tears and in
basketball titles, Grammy Awards
scholarships and jail cells.

We are also the Jezebel
the booty, the re-definers of
fashion.

This body boldly states
no earrings are too big
no color to loud
no dance move I cannot make.

Is this the female body
The Black female body.

Back to the topic of the word whore

The one you lust after
The one you want to stake your
Territory
To claim to own to use to subordinate

Not a whore but not sexless
We weave in the middle of the two
Tides low with all my coral hanging out
Waving seaweed aroma of fish

Behind her back

they say she has it too easy on account of that hair, straight and good, but she is looking envious at the love they have for each other one says to her mother "is she single" but she knows the answer. it's yes. she was just waiting for the cue. I know why she says. black men don't want her cuz she's too light. white men don't want her because she's too dark. this is about marriage not the other thing called lust. which is where exotic and good hair fit in. behind her back they say, she thinks she's better than us is it her or them or society that breaks the bond because wherever you look there she is smiling and jiving and she acts like a house or a horse or a whore they all blend together under skin that is too dark be transparent and too light to be worthy of notice.

Not White Enough, My Brother

That conversation when
He said,
"I'm so glad I found you,
we found each other—I know how hard it
is for Black women to find a Black man."

Why did he say that?
When he chose a white girl in the end
My mulatto voice says—you weren't even white enough.

Angela

I was a hippie child when Angela Davis
strode in tall and glittering golden
alongside Stokely Carmichael.
I can only remember a lobby
        a Virgo beautiful, tiny book
        miniature Renaissance castles
                peasants working in fields.
A ten point plan.

Angela spent
        a long time with me that night.
        told me many secrets, about equality,
        decent education and ending police brutality
        through astrological fairy tales.

I fell in love with her that night when she signed my book which I still have.
Later, I grew up and studied about her in college,
read her books when I became conscious of myself as a Black woman in America.

In my early twenties, I had a chance to see her speak at an event in Oakland.
I rushed backstage to meet her.
I wanted to remind her of that quiet night in Honolulu in the 1970s.

When the moment came—my words were lost—but her eyes reminded me of
        Black is beautiful, Self-love and self-liberation,
            A calling to action.

Why do Black People Protest?

Black people have always fought for this country.
Fought this country
Alongside whites, occupying spaces of shadow.

My grandfather's hat and gun, crossbow, spurs,
Twinkle in his matted eye. Hair like a Buffalo
Soldier's.
In the bedroom too is silence.

The stop. The choking gall to aspire towards light.
Of course a synthetic illusion of freedom.
Please hold my blistered cotton hand, love.
Open the door, there's a baked ham on the front table.

But to sacrifice my happiness to hatred
What for? Am I obligated too, to pay
Price paid so many times over?

Arms weary from carrying the sign post
Pinched nerves in the back of the spines

I AM A WOMAN

Define: Wild Yellowtail Sushi

Born in the aquamarine sea
Tangled in beautiful weed
flavorless , she must be broken
Hooked, decapitated
Heart wrenched out
Sliced
Placed on ice
This is when flavor forms
Her lifeless pieces on display

Race Commandments

In my own skin, I am the enemy. Contextualized in this Black vs White frame. I am a traitor. I am not Black. Am I even an ally? I evade the margins and disappear.

If one believes that being silent is worse than the actual crime, or that thinking the thought is the same as doing it. Then I am all ten sins.

I am first a murderer. I have slain myself in full and in part, denying life first to one half of myself and then to the other.

 A covetous robber, I have taken the lord god's name as a weapon to smite my enemy, especially when god wore blue jeans (eyes) and walked in wolf's clothing inside my house to take what he wanted including my body which I gave willingly a sacrifice for worship to him.

The one sin from which I find absolution is a matter of semen/tics—for how can I have committed adultery without coveting my neighbor's... but he was not a wife, just kept, passive, a possession.

I have dishonored both mother and father and that is a story I will live to tell. It is on this Lord's day that I bear this false witness. In writing these words, my prayer is to be absolved

I am a race trader (traitor)
When I was born, they would have called me a Black baby, but I traded that in for *beautiful baby girl.*
At some point, I became Black and white baby
eventually passing for Hawaiian
I evolved to I don't give a fuck what you think teenager
Beautiful long legs, long wavy, silky hair
Never says no to anything dare devil girl
In college, I was exotic girl from Hawaii
Pretty for a Black girl
Not like the others
Not really Black or white girl, girl
I became flying by, running through,
I became runner girl, stalker girl, barefoot, panty less
Snoring girl
I became

Girl who had seizures, with black eye, sleeping in class and though exams girl
I became what am I? girl,
What are you girl?
Mixed up
Mixed race
Victim of rape
Not survivor girl

I became yellow girl
Wanna be white girl
Passing girl
Poet

I became who are you? girl

Eventually I became a woman
Mother, not so Black as her daughter
Abandoned
Single
I became Black woman

I became Black woman in Africa
Not Black African woman
Murungu in Africa
Black teacher
Not Black enough teacher
Not real Black teacher
I became woman angry,
Angry Black woman
too much Black/White
not enough Black/White

I became dance poet
I became poet teacher
I became forgive me mother
Forgive me father
I became me, mother
I became and am becoming
me
I
am
me

Karla Brundage is a Bay Area based poet, activist, and educator with a passion for social justice. Born in Berkeley, California in the summer of love to a Black mother and white father, Karla spent most of her childhood in Hawaii where she developed a deep love of nature. A Pushcart Prize nominee, Fulbright teacher she has performed her work onstage and online, both nationally and internationally. Her poetry, short stories and essays can be found in *Tribes, Konch, Hip Mama, sPARKLE & bLINK, Bamboo Ridge Press,* and *WriteNow*. She is the founder of West Oakland to West Africa Poetry Exchange (WO2WA), which has facilitated cross-cultural exchange between Oakland and West African poets and the publication of three books *Our Spirits Carry Our Voices, Sisters Across Oceans* and B*lack Rootedness: 54 Poets from Africa to America*. Her musical loves include Hawaiian, West African, and Hip Hop sounds. Her work can be found at http://westoaklandtowestafrica.com/ as well as on https://www.karlabrundage.com/.

www.ingramcontent.com/pod-product-compliance
Lightning Source LLC
Chambersburg PA
CBHW020341170426
43200CB00006B/458